WITHDRAWN

MOTION

A Buddy Book

by

Julie Murray

VISIT US AT
www.abdopublishing.com

Published by ABDO Publishing Company, 4940 Viking Drive, Edina, Minnesota 55435.

Copyright © 2007 by Abdo Consulting Group, Inc. International copyrights reserved in all countries. No part of this book may be reproduced in any form without written permission from the publisher. Buddy Books™ is a trademark and logo of ABDO Publishing Company.

Printed in the United States.

Series Coordinator: Sarah Tieck
Contributing Editor: Michael P. Goecke
Graphic Design: Maria Hosley
Cover Photograph: Photos.com
Interior Photographs/Illustrations: Clipart.com, Media Bakery, Photos.com

Library of Congress Cataloging-in-Publication Data

Murray, Julie, 1969–
    Motion / Julie Murray.
        p. cm. — (First science)
    Includes index.
    ISBN-13: 978-1-59679-829-8
    ISBN-10: 1-59679-829-7
    1. Motion—Juvenile literature. I. Title. II. Series: Murray, Julie, 1969- First Science.

QC133.5 M88 2006
531'.11—dc22

                                          2006017168

TABLE OF CONTENTS

FACTS IN MOTION

Motion is a big part of everyday life. It is easy to see motion in action in many places. Just look around! When a person is running, he or she is in motion. When a car drives by, it is in motion. When someone throws a baseball through the air, the baseball is in motion.

When a person throws a snowball, the snowball is in motion.

THE SCIENCE OF MOTION

Motion happens when an object changes its position in space. When something is in motion, people say that it is moving. Speed describes how fast an object is moving.

When a paper airplane is flying, air resistance can slow it down.

When an object is moving, **force** is what helps slow it down or speed it up. **Friction** is a kind of force. So is **resistance** from air or other objects.

HOW MOTION WORKS

In the late 1600s, scientist Sir Isaac Newton came up with three laws of motion. These laws help explain his ideas about how motion works.

Newton's first law says that an object in motion tends to keep moving. It also says that an object not in motion tends to keep still. This is called **inertia**.

A ball that is stopped will stay still until someone moves it.

It takes some kind of **force** to change an object's motion. For example, a ball doesn't move until a person throws it. When the ball is moving, it will keep moving until it hits the ground or a person catches it.

A ball that is moving will keep moving until something stops it. This might be a person catching the ball or friction from the ground.

Newton's second law describes how **force** changes an object's motion. This change is called **acceleration**.

Change in acceleration depends on two things. The first is how much **mass** or weight an object has. The second is how much force was applied to the object.

Newton created a formula to show this. The formula is $F = ma$. F stands for "force." M refers to the "mass" of the object. A is for "acceleration." This formula helps people measure the acceleration, or change in motion.

A person hitting a ball with a racket shows Newton's second law.

Newton's third law is about action and reaction. This law states that for each action, there is an equal and opposite reaction, or response.

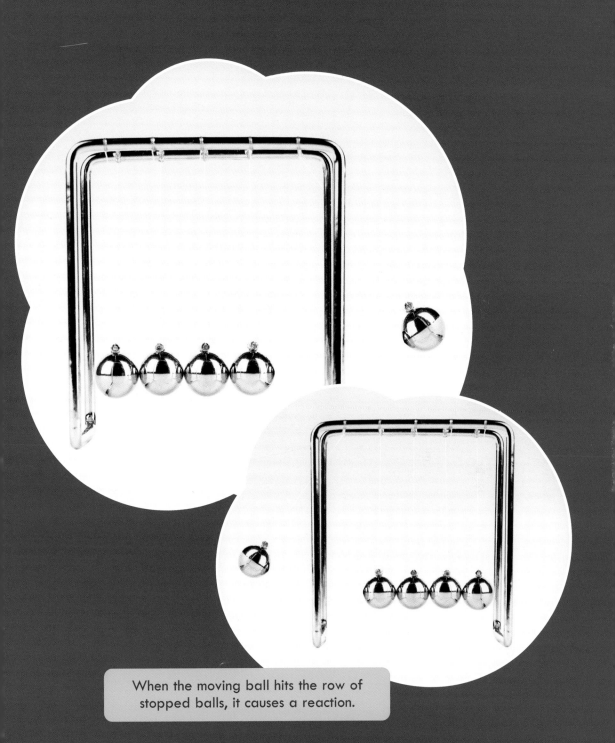

When the moving ball hits the row of stopped balls, it causes a reaction.

Moving cars are an example of motion in action. Cars move people from place to place.

Pressing the **accelerator** pedal speeds up a car. This allows it to move faster. Pushing on the brake pedal slows down or stops the car. These pedals allow the driver to control the car's speed and motion.

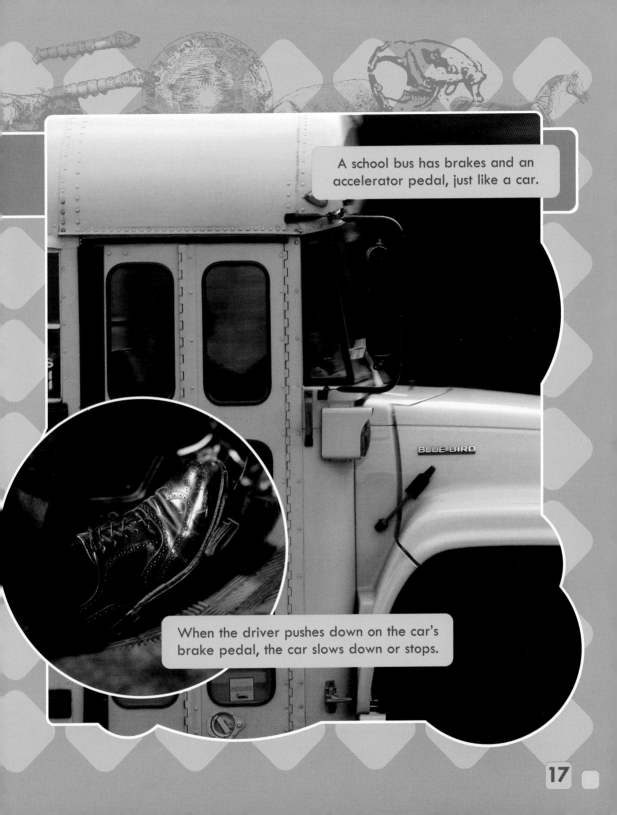

A school bus has brakes and an accelerator pedal, just like a car.

When the driver pushes down on the car's brake pedal, the car slows down or stops.

MOVING THROUGH HISTORY

Through the years, many scientists have tried to understand the science of motion.

One of the most famous people to study motion is Sir Isaac Newton. In 1687, he published his laws of motion. These laws helped him explain his ideas about motion to other people.

Sir Isaac Newton

Since Newton came up with his laws of motion, many people have studied motion. They've made important discoveries. Still, most people agree there is much more to learn about this science.

The Earth is in a constant state of motion.

.. MOTION IN THE WORLD TODAY ..

Motion is a big part of daily life. Without motion, planets wouldn't **orbit** the sun. People wouldn't be able to travel on an airplane. Without motion, people wouldn't be able to go bowling, either.

The world would be a very different place without motion.

Without motion, people wouldn't be able to swing.

IMPORTANT WORDS

acceleration to increase in speed.

force anything that changes the movement of something else.

friction a force that slows motion when two surfaces touch each other.

inertia the tendency of an object to stay in motion if it is moving, or to remain at rest if it is at rest.

mass an amount of something.

orbit the path of a planet as it moves around another planet.

resistance something that works against or opposes.

WEB SITES

To learn more about **Motion**, visit ABDO Publishing Company on the World Wide Web. Web site links about **Motion** are featured on our Book Links page. These links are routinely monitored and updated to provide the most current information available.

www.abdopublishing.com

.. INDEX ..